R. R. Conn

Human moral problem:

An inquiry into some of the dark points connected with the human necessities for a supernatural savior

R. R. Conn

Human moral problem:
An inquiry into some of the dark points connected with the human necessities for a supernatural savior

ISBN/EAN: 9783337817886

Hergestellt in Europa, USA, Kanada, Australien, Japan

Cover: Foto ©ninafisch / pixelio.de

Weitere Bücher finden Sie auf **www.hansebooks.com**

THE
HUMAN MORAL PROBLEM

An Enquiry

INTO

SOME OF THE DARK POINTS CONNECTED WITH
THE HUMAN NECESSITIES FOR A
SUPERNATURAL SAVIOUR

BY

R. R. CONN

NEW YORK
A. C. ARMSTRONG AND SON
1889

INTRODUCTION.

THE writer of the following pages is a layman. He has had no instruction in theological subjects beyond what he has gained in reading theological discussions and in listening to the utterances from evangelical pulpits for fifty years. During one of these years he had the privilege of listening to the preaching of the talented Charles G. Finney. All this has left on his mind a certain amount of dissatisfaction with the way in which have been presented some points connected with the human moral disabilities, and the human moral necessities for a supernatural Saviour. The writer would claim no more weight for his thoughts than the thoughts of one in his position deserve; yet it may be of interest to the pulpit to know how its utterances sometimes strike listeners.

So far as the author is aware, some of the thoughts expressed in these pages are new; at least, he has never read them in any book nor heard them advanced in any pulpit. Nevertheless, he believes that they are not in conflict with the doctrines usually received as evangelical. It is not his purpose, however, especially to defend evangelical doctrines.

The little word "sin" has been used so often by religious writers and speakers that it has come to have half a dozen different meanings. In its primary significance it seems to mean disobedience to the Creator's commands. It is, however, also used in the sense of temptation, in the sense of guilt, in the sense of depravity, in the sense of shortcomings resulting from weakness, in the sense of the weakness of infirmity, and in the abstract sense of that which is forbidden before it becomes associated with the subject and has any guilt adhering to it. A word with so many meanings becomes too indefinite for close logical discussion. For this reason the author will not use the word "sin." For the last of the meanings given above he will use the term "the forbidden." This phrase will occur quite often. It has a negative as well as a positive sense,— that of omission as well as that of commission.

The earth has many problems. They pervade the organic and the inorganic world. Prominent among them is found the moral problem. The earth has a moral problem because its supreme creature, man, has a moral nature. A moral nature implies the power of choice, and this power makes man in one sense a first cause, and thus a likeness of his Creator.

The general features of the moral problem must be the same in all worlds where moral beings are found. The earth probably has a moral problem with special features, because man has a nature peculiar in itself. But this we cannot prove, because the Creator has not seen fit to let us know whether he has placed moral beings on the other orbs of the universe; nor can we know whether these beings, if they do exist, are any or all of them like man. From what we see of the general diversity of the Creator's works, we may assume that moral beings with the peculiar nature of man would not be found in other worlds. The offering of the Saviour for man, though supernatural to the highest degree, even to the union of God and man in one person, seems to be a feature pertaining to this earth. He represents the remedial plan for no other kind of moral beings, but man.

Our discussion will notice the disability found in man, called depravity. This disability the Creator did not originally place in man. He gave him a plastic nature, whereby it was possible for him to bring depravity upon himself by disobedience to his Creator. Man has very generally availed himself of this grim privilege, and depravity is a great factor in the human moral problem. The distinctive feature of depravity is that it produces in man some inclination to do what is destructive to himself. It will be the attempt of our discussion, however, to show that depravity is not the only disability in man producing the inclination to do what will bring upon him his destruction. We shall endeavor to prove that there is another disability, more fundamental and of a greater magnitude than the self-made one of depravity. It was found in the first Adam before the advent of depravity into the world, and it was present also in the second Adam, whose nature was never defiled by depravity. In our discussion this second disability is by far the more important and fundamental; but the author does not remember ever to have seen the thought in any work on systematic theology, or to have heard it in any sermon.

Man has so generally become guilty and gone astray, that to meet his necessities a Saviour was necessary who would be able to blot out his past guilt. But the blotting out of past guilt, though so indispensable, is not, as we shall attempt to show, his greatest or his fundamental necessity for a supernatural Saviour. It is a greater necessity that his future should be free from guilt. The future is made free from guilt by prevention, the past by cure. It is a good physician who can cure, but it is a greater physician who can prevent disease. The God-man, when he gives man strength and victory in times of temptation, is greater than when he forgives man for past offences, and simply removes the guilt and penalty. The former is salvation, the latter is only a means toward it, and only valuable as it contributes toward it. Strength to resist the evil tendencies in man's nature is man's greatest necessity. This necessity existed before the advent into the world of any guilt, and human nature is not equal to it. If we could find some one who had always remained guiltless, instead of finding in him one who had no necessity for a Saviour, we should find one in whom was exemplified the highest and the most perfect type of salvation through the power of the Saviour. These pages will enlarge on this necessity, because the author has listened to so many sermons in which it was left out, and the necessity of forgiveness made the all in all. How often is the statement made that man is a sinner; and this is given as the only reason why man needs a Saviour! There is a strange absurdity growing out of this position. It is conceded by all that " there is no other name given under heaven whereby man can be saved" but that of Jesus Christ. If the salvation of Christ is the salvation of sinners only, the conception of one who did not become a sinner would be the conception of one who could not be saved, since there would be no avenue through which such a Saviour could reach him; thus disobedience and guilt would become necessities to salvation. The author has seen persons who held this theory of salvation, grow very impatient and almost angry with one suggesting that that there might be those who would grow into obedience as they grow into accountability, and never become sinners. To admit such a possibility would take away the key-stone to their theory of salvation, and would let it fall into absurdity.

It is not our purpose to inquire as to whether such cases ever do occur; but to contend for a theory of salvation which will still hold if there shall ever be such a thing as a guiltless person.

The method of questions and answers has been adopted in the discussion in order to give clearness and point, and to use the least possible number of words.

FITCHBURG, MASS.

THE HUMAN MORAL PROBLEM.

THE FORBIDDEN.

1. *Q.* Who is the rightful Sovereign of the earth?
   A. The Creator.

2. *Q.* What is the all-important creature of earth?
   A. Man.

3. *Q.* Why is man the all-important creature of earth?
   A. Because he is created in the image of his Creator.

4. *Q.* In what does this resemblance consist?
   A. God is a spirit; man has a spiritual nature. God is an intellectual being; man has an intellect. God has sensibility; man has the same. God is a moral being with freedom of choice; man is a moral being with freedom of choice. First cause is said to be an attribute of the Creator; man through his power of choice can bring about events without the necessity of an external cause, and may therefore in a sense be said to be a first cause.

5. *Q.* Do all elements of earth contribute to man's success?

A. No; though there is enough to insure success if rightly chosen. There is much that may be chosen which only conspires to man's ruin.

6. *Q.* Why did the Creator give man the power of choosing evil as well as good?

A. This is the necessary outcome of his free agency; one of the attributes in which he is the image of his Creator.

7. *Q.* What did man's rightful Sovereign do for him on account of the disastrous possibilities of his free agency amid the destructive elements of earth?

A. He forbade man to taste or even touch the destructive elements.

8. *Q.* Why did the Creator thus forbid man?

A. Because it would be another inducement to man to go in the right direction.

9. *Q.* Does the prohibition of God prevent man from choosing the evil?

A. Not necessarily; because man is free to choose, and in that respect is his own sovereign.

10. *Q.* Why was it necessary to forbid man to partake of what was destructive to him, the presumption being that he would not choose to do what would insure his own destruction?

A. In the first instance, man is supposed to be ignorant of the fact that some things are destructive, and the prohibition would instruct him. But this is not all. Much that is destructive is also attractive, and the prohibition of God is a force tending to offset this attractiveness.

11. *Q.* Has not the Creator given attractiveness to those elements that contribute to man's well being?

A. He has.

12. *Q.* Is the attractiveness of the destructive and the life-giving the same in kind?

A. They resemble each other in some respects, but not in all.

13. *Q.* In what are they in contrast?

A. The life-giving, that which is the right, that which the Creator commands to be done, that which, when done, is virtue, always promises a final good; but the destructive, that which the forbidden is, that which done is disobedience, can only promise evil and disaster as its final result.

14. *Q.* In what do they resemble each other?

A. Both at times produce immediate pleasure, and at others they do not; both also at times produce immediate pain or discomfort.

15. *Q.* When the right and the wrong are pitted against each other for choice, do these resemblances always appear?

A. By no means. One may offer an immediate pleasure, while the other can offer only immediate pain or evil.

16. *Q.* What is the effect when such is the case?

A. When the right can offer immediate pleasure and the wrong cannot prevent immediate pain or evil, the safety of man is complete; but when the reverse is the case, as frequently happens, and the wrong can offer immediate pleasure, and the right can only offer immediate pain or self-denial, then comes the peril of human existence. Here is brought to view one of the fundamental factors of the human moral problem.

17. *Q.* Does the forbidden never produce pleasure beyond the present?

A. When it operates through the lower passions and appetites, it evidently does not; but when it appeals to the higher nature there is some obscurity. The forbidden promises reward in the future; but there is a question whether these promised rewards are not always delusions, and the actual pleasures all confined to the anticipation of them. At any rate the pleasures of the forbidden are but for a season, and of short duration at most, to be followed by pain and bitterness.

18. *Q.* How does the final reward of virtue compare with the pleasure or good that the forbidden can insure for the present or the near future?

A. The rewards of virtue are immeasurably great both in duration and magnitude; while the most that the forbidden can do is to offer pleasures of gratification of a trifling duration or magnitude.

19. *Q.* Can the forbidden become a temptation to human nature in conflict and in contrast

with the infinite rewards of virtue, when it can offer only trifling pleasures?

A. Yes; temptations of such extreme magnitude and power as to insure disaster and ruin to the whole race of man, which can only be prevented by the supernatural interference of the Creator.

20. *Q.* Under such apparent adverse inducements, how is it possible for the forbidden thus to captivate human nature?

A. Pictures with true perspective have what are called vanishing points. An object, to be seen in the distance, must be made smaller; and the farther from the foreground it is supposed to be, the smaller it must be represented, until a point is reached in which its outline vanishes at the vanishing point, and there it is rendered invisible. Time is a picture; the present is its foreground, the future is its background. Interests impress the sensibility in the ratio of their nearness to the present. The short pleasures that the forbidden offers are in the present or are near to it, and its long woes are in the future, — sometimes in the far distant future. The trifling good that the forbidden offers is always in the foreground of time, and it eclipses the immeasurable woes that must follow, because these are so near to the vanishing points of the future. We find this principle brought out in the Scripture: " Because sentence against an evil work is not executed speedily, therefore the heart of the sons of men is fully set in them to do evil."

21. *Q.* What general attribute has human nature that is not in the image of his Creator, but

which is a factor of great magnitude in the human moral problem?

A. It is plasticity, or the susceptibility of being moulded.

22. *Q.* When did this attribute appear in human nature?

A. It is one of the original attributes of man.

23. *Q.* Why is it not one of the attributes that he received in the image of his Creator?

A. Such an attribute is impossible to God, who is unchangeable, infinite, and absolute.

24. *Q.* Why is plasticity such an important factor in the human moral problem?

A. Though not an attribute of the Creator, it enables man to develop, and reach higher and higher attainments in those attributes which he does possess in the image of his Creator.

25. *Q.* What does the fact that God created man with the susceptibility of being moulded prove?

A. That the Creator did not at first give man that high order of being which he intended for him in after time.

26. *Q.* What does the fact that God created the first pair with plastic natures prove in regard to their standard of being?

A. That as regards their positive qualities they were not a high standard for us to aim at. They were innocent, there was an absence of bad qualities, which is desirable; but this is only a negative, not a positive quality. It makes no difference with this argument whether Adam be considered as the first individual man or a type of the race of man.

27. *Q.* Is there a high human mark that is fit to be the aim of every human being?

A. Yes; there was such a standard of high quality in Jesus of Nazareth.

28. *Q.* What exceeding peril is indissolubly connected with the grand human attribute of plasticity?

A. The susceptibility of being moulded in the direction of elevation implies the same susceptibility in the direction of degradation.

29. *Q.* What can mould man in the direction of degradation?

A. Doing the forbidden.

30. *Q.* Is the degradation that is brought about by doing the forbidden, a general and equal degradation of all the powers and faculties of man?

A. No; it does not reduce the whole manhood in an equal manner. It enlarges one part at the expense of another, and so deranges and changes the functions of the different powers and faculties, that they are not what they were intended to be by the Creator.

31. *Q.* Is plasticity in man his fundamental peril?

A. No; man's tendency to do the forbidden lies underneath it.

32. *Q.* What, then, is man's fundamental peril of existence?

A. It is the fact that the forbidden may be attractive to him, together with the fact of his free moral agency.

33. *Q.* How came it about that the forbidden could be attractive to man?

A. The Creator in the first place gave to certain of the destructive elements of earth,— elements which he afterward forbade,— a nature that made them attractive to man.

34. *Q.* Did the Creator originally give to human nature any defective powers or susceptibilities?

A. No.

35. *Q.* Did the Creator give to human nature any powers or susceptibilities that could be dispensed with?

A. No; man has need of all his original powers and faculties.

36. *Q.* How was it possible that the destructive and the forbidden could have been attractive to human nature in its original normal condition, before it became degraded, and while it was still what the Creator seemed so well pleased with?

A. Man has certain indispensable wants, some of them relating to life itself and others relating to what makes life desirable. These wants are immediate and pressing, and must be met at once, or disaster will follow. Man's intellectual nature would in time have made these wants and their method of fulfilment known to him, but the action of intellect is so slow that man would have died in the interval. Hence there arises in man the necessity of something different from intellect, — something more rapid in its action, something that would impel man to his wants without the necessity of any reasoning. The Creator gave to man originally just this kind of power. It is called feeling, or instinct. Its demands are pressing and it acts promptly. It is blind, however, not being able to discriminate like the intellect. Its pure function has no more reason in it than the steel has when it tends toward the magnet. The earth is supposed to have elements enough in it to satisfy human wants; but the Creator in his wisdom placed among the life-giving elements some that were death-dealing. Nor is this all. The Creator in some cases gave to the death-dealing elements some qualities in which they resemble the life-giving; and this resemblance was so great that the blind feelings were not able to distinguish the difference between them, and desired the one as they did the other. We thus have the key to man's original susceptibility to sin, — the fact that human sensibility or feeling was not of sufficient refinement and of a sufficiently high order to distinguish completely between the life-giving and the death-giving elements of nature.

37. *Q.* Could man have had a nature that was not susceptible to temptation?

A. He could; the only question would be whether he would still be man if he had such a nature.

38. *Q.* Why, then, is man subject to temptation?

A. Because his strength is not equal to his environment.

NORMAL AND ABNORMAL DISABILITY.

39. *Q.* What is often mistaken for and confounded with human depravity?

A. Human weakness.

40. *Q.* What is weakness, and what is strength?

A. The Almighty is the only being who is devoid of weakness. Man is weak and strong according to his surroundings; if he is equal to them he is strong, if not he is weak.

41. *Q.* What is the difference between **depravity** and **weakness**?

A. The same as between the child and the cripple. Weakness may exist where there is perfection in all parts, but depravity is imperfection. There is weakness where there is imperfection, so that there is weakness in depravity. But there is also weakness in the absence of depravity, for human nature may be weak when it is not depraved. It is weak at all times. Weakness is legitimate, but depravity is not. The Creator gave the original man weakness but not depravity. Weakness is natural, depravity is artificial.

42. *Q.* In what do weakness and depravity resemble each other?

A. They are both sources of human temptation.

43. *Q.* Are these sources of temptation generally independent?

A. No; they are usually associated.

44. *Q.* Are there any cases of one in the absence of the other?

A. There are cases of weakness in the absence of depravity, but never cases of depravity in the absence of weakness.

45. *Q.* What may be said of our first parents before the fall?

A. In their case we find temptations caused by weakness in the absence of depravity.

46. *Q.* What may be said of the strength of Jesus our Saviour?

A. We believe Jesus to have had two natures, that of the Deity and that of man. The first is almighty, and there is no weakness possible to it. If this part of the nature of Jesus had been shown in its full power, it would have changed the weakness of his human nature to the almightiness of the Deity. To be human he must have been weak, though he might have been the strongest being of earth at that time or of any future time. One purpose of his advent seemed to be to suffer temptations as we do. His human nature was not imperfect or degraded. It could be weak and perfect at the same time. Unless it was weak in comparison to almightiness, it could not have been susceptible to temptation. At the same time in comparison to the strength of other men he was strong, for he spake as never man spake before or since.

47. *Q.* How could Jesus be tempted like as we are?

A. Whatever different schools teach in regard to human depravity, they agree in the belief that Jesus was free from every shade of it. He could therefore have suffered none of the temptations that are caused by depravity. It is difficult to see how he could be tempted like as we are, to an extent that could be called human, on any other ground than that the temptations whose origin is human weakness are generic, and those whose origin is depravity are exceptional and temporary.

48. *Q.* Is human weakness a larger factor in the temptations of mankind than human depravity?

A. Yes; we say it is, and shall try to prove it in the substance of what follows.

49. *Q.* Which of the two causes brought temptation into the world?

A. Human weakness.

50. *Q.* Why could not human depravity be the original cause of human temptation to do the forbidden?

A. Because doing the forbidden is the cause of depravity, and must antedate it. But the temptation must always antedate the actual doing of the forbidden, and therefore the depravity of human nature could not be the original cause of temptation.

51. *Q.* What was the origin of human weakness?

A. Strength and weakness are relative terms. The Creator in the first place did not give man a sufficiently high order of being, or, in other words, sufficient strength to be above being tempted by the forbidden things of the world in which he was to live.

52. *Q.* What was the origin of human depravity?

A. The Creator in the first place gave man a plastic nature and the power of choice. By abusing both of these grand attributes man became the cause of his own depravity. Primarily, the Creator is the cause of human weakness, and man is the cause of human depravity.

53. *Q.* Does the advent of depravity extinguish that original weakness which was the foundation of man's susceptibility to temptation?

A. No; such a position would be absurd. Wrong-doing is the cause of depravity; it always tends to disability, to evil, to death, and it is absurd to speak of it as removing weakness. Its whole tendency is the other way. Wrong-doing cannot in any sense extinguish human weakness, for that would be a good. It is forbidden by the Creator for the very reason that it promotes evil and not good. If the human weakness that produces the susceptibility to temptation does ever become reduced in man's nature, it is done in spite of human depravity, by virtue of well-doing, — the same cause that tends to reduce depravity.

54. *Q.* Was there any force that could extinguish man's original susceptibility to temptation at the time that depravity entered the world?

A. This original susceptibility depended upon the original strength or weakness with which the Creator saw fit to invest human nature. It was no slight quality, and no slight force could remove it. It entered so radically into the very substance of human nature, that no power short of a creative miracle could suddenly change man to a degree that would extinguish it. This susceptibility was present in the human nature of Jesus our Saviour. It is absurd to expect not to find it in natures that are imperfect and of less strength.

55. *Q.* What is the logical inference of all this?

A. That man's original susceptibility to temptation is a factor still in operation in the temptations of all men; that the additional factor, depravity, which is a new and second source of temptation, does not necessitate the departure of the original and first; that both are factors in the temptation of man as we know him.

56. *Q.* Is it possible that man, through his plastic nature, can ever reach a degree of strength that will place him above the susceptibility to temptation?

A. There seems to be a logical difficulty in answering this question either way. If we knew that the forbidden things of earth were of a fixed and positive nature, the logic of human plasticity would demand a degree of positive strength that would match them. It may be that the forbidden is plastic too, and that it will expand with the strength of higher attainments, and that man, as he ascends to new plains, will find new fields of forbidden fruits. Our limited experience looks that way but does not prove it. We know that the Master, with his superior nature, was tempted. We shall therefore assume the negative, which seems to have the preponderance of evidence. The logical connection of our subject is not affected by either answer. We shall attempt to prove soon that there is a possibility of the destruction of depravity, and consequently of the temptation caused by it.

57. *Q.* If we have made the logical deductions correctly, what error has been made in much religious teaching?

A. Depravity has frequently been made the sole factor in temptation since the fall of man.

THE TRANSMISSION OF DISABILITY.

58. *Q.* Do the laws of human plasticity limit man's power to himself?

A. No; a parent who has moulded his own nature by good or evil doing may transmit a moulded nature to his offspring.

59. *Q.* Are the mouldings that a parent may give his children certain and uniform?

A. No; though the general law is fixed that the child inherits his nature from his parents.

60. *Q.* What is the cause of so much uncertainty?

A. There are two parents and four grandparents, and thus there are several forces that may operate to make up the child. Sometimes one force predominates, and sometimes another. They may be antagonistic and counteract each other, or they may be such that a general blending takes place and no distinct inherited peculiarity is visible. Doubtless there is a definite and regular law underneath the seeming confusion, but our knowledge is not sufficient to fathom it.

61. *Q.* What is the final limit beyond which such qualities are not inherited?

A. There seems to be an intimation of this limit in the second commandment, in which God says that he visits the iniquities of the fathers on the third and fourth generations. So far as we can tell, science and general observation seem to indicate that single peculiarities of a single individual cannot be transmitted for many generations.

62. *Q.* If this is the law, how can we account for those cases where the same tendencies are visible in line of descent for more than four generations?

A. Children are liable to act in the direction of inherited tendencies. Such actions would mould their natures in the direction of these tendencies if they had not already inherited them. As it is, the tendencies are strengthened. This strengthening is thus going on through the actions of the successive individuals at the same time that the inherited tendencies should be fading out. The strengthening may be equal to the fading, and thus the same tendencies may be kept alive indefinitely through a long line of natural descent. It is like a child's hoop that continues to roll after the force of the first blow is spent, by the blows that follow. Thus depravity has rolled down upon us from the ages by the continued wrong-doing of the successive generations of man, though the force of the first blow that was given to it by the first parents was spent long ago.

63. *Q.* What distinction is it necessary, at this stage of our inquiry, to protect with the utmost care?

A. The distinction between man's natural and his acquired qualities; between those attributes that the Creator originally gave him, which are necessary to him as a human being, and with which he cannot part and still be a human being, and those changes that are made possible through his original attribute of plasticity.

64. *Q.* Why is it so important to protect this distinction?

A. Because the manner in which the two classes are transmitted by parents to their children are so radically different.

65. *Q.* We have inquired into the laws by which parents transmit acquired qualities to their issue. By what laws do they transmit those qualities that are original and cannot be acquired?

A. Moses answers this in his history of creation. He says that the Creator commanded each to produce after his kind. According to this law every human parent must transmit to his offspring all of those qualities that are distinctively human.

66. *Q.* Were the first parents unique as to the plasticity of their nature?

A. No; the Creator gave to our first parents a plastic nature, and said that they should produce after their kind. This implies that they should produce in their issue all the attributes that the Creator gave them, and they therefore could not have possessed any unique attributes of the original kind, but were plastic like the rest of us.

67. *Q.* What does this fact prove?

A. That the first parents were not unique in their susceptibility to depravity.

68. *Q.* Were the first parents unique as to the transmission of their acquired attributes to their issue?

A. No; the Creator gave our first parents certain laws by which they could transmit their acquired qualities to their issue. The Creator said that they should produce after their kind, — which means that they should produce issue bound by the same laws of production that the Creator gave to them. Therefore they must have transmitted their acquired qualities to issue in just the same manner that other human parents do.

69. *Q.* What does this last fact prove?

A. That the first parents had no more power, as parents, to transmit the depravity of the fall to their issue, than other human parents have since had to transmit their depravity to their issue.

70. *Q.* Were our first parents unique as to their connection with human depravity in any respect?

A. They were unique in being the first ones to bring depravity into the world. This does not signify much. They were first in other matters too.

71. *Q.* To what degree could our first parents transmit the depravity of the fall to their issue?

A. We have seen that human parents cannot transmit their acquired qualities through many generations. The first parents, not being unique in this respect, might have transmitted the depravity of the fall to their issue for a few generations, but not more.

72. *Q.* What absurd state of things would have existed in our world if our first parents had had the power to transmit the depravity of the fall to all generations, as is taught by some theologians?

A. All human parents would have had the same power as the first parents, or they would not have been after the kind of the first. All the iniquities of that portion of the race that became parents, and whose lines did not become extinct, would have been visited upon the present generations of our world. Cain's murderous depravity would have followed his descendants to the present day. If we can take the flood as literally destroying the entire race of men, except Noah's family, then Noah would become the father of all those living since his time, as well as Adam. Noah was something of a drunkard, and therefore whatever of a drunkard's depravity he brought upon himself must be visited upon all living at the present time. When we take into account, in addition, the fact of so many drunkards in past generations, and the improbability that the lines of none of us could have escaped crossing with some drunkard, there would have been something more than a probability that every one of us would have inherited a drunkard's appetite. The same logic could be followed out in other lines and kinds of depravity. Such a state of things is supremely absurd, and would have extinguished every vestige of the human race long ago.

73. *Q.* Are these laws that govern human plasticity themselves plastic?

A. No; these laws appertain to the original manhood, and it is as necessary that they should be immutable and rigid as it is that the bones of the body should be; otherwise the whole manhood would fall into chaos.

74. *Q.* Are the laws that govern human heredity plastic?

A. No; they appertain to the original manhood, and the same chaotic result would follow if they were not immutable and rigid.

75. *Q.* What effect did the fall of man have on the race of men?

A. There can be no doubt that the transgression did mould the natures of the actors to a certain degree in the direction of debasement. We have seen that the physical effects of this moulding could reach only the first few generations. There are reasons why its effect could not have been great even on the first few. One transgression could hardly mould the nature sufficiently to be appreciated in the next generation. Only a long course of trangression could greatly affect posterity. If the first parents became obedient through the power of the promised seed of woman, as soon as it was offered, the depravity that Cain and Abel would have inherited would be very slight. On the other hand, if the first parents continued on in their disobedience as they began, their subsequent acts would have produced mouldings in the direction of depravity as well as the first act of disobedience, so that the depravity that they entailed on their offspring would be mixed. Even in this case there could be only a small part of the actual depravity of the first few generations that could be chargeable to the depravity of the fall.

76. *Q*. What have many theologians claimed that the fall of our first parents did for the world?

A. That it placed in store for every one of the future race of mankind a disability or a curse.

77. *Q*. By what method do these theologians claim that this disability or curse could be fastened upon the sons of men?

A. Some of the more modern teach that the fall produced in the first parents a depraved nature, and that they fastened it upon their descendants by the laws of hereditary descent. The older theologians do not attempt to explain the method, but treat it as a fiat of the Creator.

78. *Q*. What have theologians taught us to believe was the fruit of this disability or curse?

A. The more ancient taught that the curse was a store of guilt that was made ready for and fastened upon every son of man as soon as he was born. The more modern deny this, and teach that it is a spirit of rebellion, a taste for doing the forbidden as such, that every one of the race, as they claim, finds fastened upon his nature.

79. *Q.* From what we have already seen, what shall we say of the power of the first parents in transmitting their depravity to all generations, by the laws of hereditary descent?

A. It is a logical absurdity as well as a physiological impossibility.

80. *Q.* What shall we say of the guilt of the first parents being placed in store, so as to be fastened upon every son and daughter of man as soon as born?

A. It is placing our Creator on a par with what heathen make their deities to be, — monsters of injustice and cruelty. But the theory is so much one of the past, that it does not deserve this much notice.

81. *Q.* Is there a spirit of rebellion in human nature that is so generic that it gives attractiveness to the destructive elements of earth simply because the Creator has made them forbidden?

A. This cannot be, for two reasons.

82. *Q.* What is the first reason?

A. If the attractiveness that the destructive things of earth have for human nature is founded on the fact that the Creator made them forbidden, then all that is forbidden should be attractive to every individual of the race. Common observation teaches that this is not so. Though perhaps there is nothing that is forbidden that does not find some nature to which it is attractive, there is no nature that finds everything that is forbidden attractive to it.

83. *Q.* What is the second reason?

A. If the attractive quality of the forbidden is the fact that it is forbidden, then the Creator made a great mistake in making it so. This would give man new inducements to partake of the destructive and the deadly. This is absurd. The Creator did not give the commandments for the purpose of adding to man's inducements to the destructive and the deadly, but as counter-inducements. And these commandments have always been counter-inducements.

84. *Q.* What then are we forced to believe?

A. That the claim made by some theologians, that there is in human nature a general spirit of rebellion against God that makes us delight in being disobedient for its own sake, is not true.

85. *Q.* Can there be found a sufficient cause for all of the evil tendencies of our kind, without a resort to any claimed curse from the fall?

A. Yes; man's evil tendencies are all comprised in his temptations to do the forbidden. We have seen that there are two sources of these temptations, — the original and the acquired. The temptations of Jesus were wholly of the original class; for no one would think for a moment of his nature being warped by the fall. These temptations were the more generic and important part of human temptations, and have no part or lot in any claimed curse that comes to us from the fall. If we exclude from the problem all those temptations in which Jesus was tempted like as we are, we shall have a remainder that is not as great as is generally supposed. And this remainder can all be charged to the depravity that men bring upon themselves, and transmit as parents to their immediate posterity. There would be nothing left to be charged to any claimed curse from the fall.

86. *Q.* What other factor of much magnitude do we find in the problem of man's evil tendencies?

A. We have thus far treated the attractiveness of the forbidden as a simple and a single force; but the forbidden has often more than one point of attractiveness. There were three attractive points in the forbidden fruit of early nativity, — it was good for food, pleasant to the eye, and desirable to make one wise.

87. *Q.* Are all the features of the forbidden attractive?

A. Never to the original and undepraved nature. It is quite a question whether depravity in its worst form can remove from the forbidden all its repellent points.

88. *Q.* What were the repellent points of the forbidden fruit of Paradise?

A. The knowledge that the fruit was deadly, and that the Creator had made it forbidden. The half belief in the lie of the tempter reduced the first of these points in a measure.

89. *Q.* In the case of any forbidden thing, do all the forces, both attractive and repellent, have a natural connection with the thing itself?

A. No; rewards and punishments are always forces outside of the case. When the Creator forbade the doing of certain destructive things, he added an external force upon the repellent side. The prohibition had no natural connection with the case.

90. *Q.* How great may be the magnitude of these external forces?

A. So great as to overmatch and destroy the freedom of the will, — that is, the freedom of the will in any particular case. Man is finite in all his powers; his free agency is one of those powers, and therefore his free agency is finite, and there may be a power, even of the finite, that can overmatch it. In such cases responsibility and guilt cease. The science of moral philosophy and theology may be slow to admit this. The science of jurisprudence, however, teaches it as a fundamental principle, and coins the law terms, intimidation, undue influence, and duress. The proof of intimidation or duress in obtaining the signature to a legal instrument takes away the responsibility of the person whose signature it is. The presumption in law is, that the person in that case had his free agency overmatched, and it was for this reason inoperative.

91. *Q.* What is one natural inference from this subject?

A. It explains how the undepraved may in any given case be tempted as severely as the depraved. While the depraved have a kind of force in their temptations that is not felt by the undepraved, the undepraved may have a peculiar environment that will produce in them temptations equal in degree, if not in kind, to those felt by the depraved. Kleptomania is an emanation of pure depravity; it is an appetite for hiding and stealing for its own sake. A person who has perfect freedom from such an appetite, and to whom thieving is repellent, may be placed in a peculiar position where much wealth may be obtained by a dishonesty which is equivalent to breaking the eighth commandment. He may then be tempted to steal in a degree equal to the impulse of the kleptomaniac, and he may yield, and be confined in the same cell with him; and yet one would be burdened with a depraved appetite and the other would not. The same subject might be followed out in other lines of depravity with the same result.

92. *Q.* What is a second inference from this subject?

A. That our Saviour, though undepraved, might be tempted in all points equally with depraved men. The temptations of the depraved proceed in great measure from a force within themselves. The undepraved have, to be sure, within themselves the susceptibility to temptation, but the moving force of their temptation proceeds from without. This was so with Jesus. His environment, we may say, was miraculously suited to produce terrible temptations that seem not only to be equal to, but greater than those of any other man. Jesus seems to have suffered, though undepraved, a degree of temptation that would have crushed into insanity or idiocy the physical as well as the moral natures of most men, — perhaps the strongest man.

93. *Q.* Is it possible for any of the race of men to be so organized and under such favorable environment, while on earth, as to be free from all temptations to do the forbidden?

A. It is true that the factors in human temptations vary in different persons, and that some are more severely tempted than others; it might seem reasonable, therefore, that there could be men so favorably situated as to all the factors that they would be entirely free from temptation. Our knowledge of mankind shows us, however, that there is no such case.

94. *Q.* What persons and conditions would seem to be the best situated for such a result?

A. The first man and woman in the garden of Eden. Their natures were free from all unfavorable biases; everything that heart could wish was in abundance before them, and yet they were tempted to partake of what was forbidden.

95. *Q.* What fact proves that the Creator's original intention was that mankind should suffer temptations in the flesh?

A. The fact that he planted the forbidden tree in paradise, and made it attractive to the natures that he intended man and woman to have.

96. *Q.* What did the Creator know would be the consequence of thus subjecting the human race to temptation?

A. He knew that he would be exposing the race to a peril of the greatest magnitude.

97. *Q.* Would the forbidden be a source of peril to man even if it were not a temptation?

A. It would. The forbidden is the death-dealing, and it is a peril to be in the midst of the death-dealing elements, even if they are repulsive.

98. *Q.* Since the Creator has seen fit to make the forbidden attractive to man, what is the effect on man's peril?

A. It is immeasurably increased.

99. *Q.* What peculiar peril is connected with the first temptation?

A. A course of action in a child may produce a habit that will add force to the first temptation, though the course of action had no guilt about it, for the reason that it was previous to the dawn of responsibility.

100. *Q.* What peculiar peril is connected with the first transgression?

A. It plants the seeds of corruption in the nature which cannot be eradicated, but will spread till the whole nature is a mass of corruption, unless there is an interference of deific power.

101. *Q.* From what we have seen thus far of the magnitude and peculiar complication of human disability and peril, what must we believe would become of the human race?

A. That it would not gain higher moral attainments, but that it would go downward from one degree of degradation to another, until all that was the image of God had become extinct, and possibly life itself.

102. *Q.* Why did such a direful state of things not come to pass?

A. Because the Creator, through the most wonderful miracle that the world ever saw, provided a plan to prevent it.

103. *Q.* When was that saving plan made known to man?

A. Not until man had yielded to temptation, and was actually going in the course of degradation.

104. *Q.* Was this plan an afterthought brought out by the sight of man in his impending ruin?

A. No; afterthoughts are not possible to the Infinite One. The plan of man's salvation was as early in divine conception as that of man's creation.

105. *Q.* Why was the offer of this saving plan withheld until man was actually in the downward course to destruction?

A. This plan has many phases, and some of them could not be appreciated until after the overt act of disobedience. It is salvation, which man cannot appreciate until he is lost; it is redemption, which man cannot understand until he has felt the galling chains of a degraded nature; it is a washing away of guilt, which man cannot realize until he is loathing his guiltiness; it is strength to resist temptation, but this does not appear in its full value till man has become weakened and broken under the power of temptation.

106. *Q.* What was the overt act of disobedience that was committed previous to the revelation of the Creator's wonderful plan for saving man?

A. It was the first disobedience, whether that be regarded as a single act or as a type of disobedience.

107. *Q.* What was there about our first parents of sufficient importance to enable them

to commit the overt act for the whole race of men?

A. This pair, or as we usually say, Adam, was chosen as a representative for the whole race of man.

MAN'S FIRST OFFICIAL REPRESENTATIVE.

108. *Q.* Who chose Adam to this official position?
A. The Creator.

109. *Q.* What were his qualifications for such an important office?
A. He was the only man who was as the Creator made him, and not a man moulded through his plastic nature in the line of disability.

110. *Q.* What seems to have been the purpose of the Creator in choosing the one man Adam to represent the individuals of the race of man?
A. To try him with temptations and to present the general temper and tendencies of the race of man as to the matter of temptations, and the necessity of a Saviour.

111. *Q.* What would the trial of the artificial disabilities of any one man show as to the general tendencies of the whole race of man?
A. Nothing; because such disabilities are special and inconstant.

112. *Q.* What kind of disabilities must be tried to bring out general truths in regard to the whole race of man?
A. Those disabilities that were present in man before the advent of depravity; those disabilities that

are inherent in human nature; that the Creator placed in man as a fixture; and that were present in the God-man, who was devoid of all kinds and shades of depravity.

113. *Q.* Why would Adam have been an unfit man to represent the whole race of man, if he had been depraved at the time of his official trial?

A. We have seen that the purpose of the trial was to set forth a general truth in regard to every man, as to his connection with the perils of temptation, and the necessity for a Saviour. We have also seen that the trial of artificial disabilities or human depravity would not set forth any general truth in regard to the whole race, and that only a trial of man's original and fixed disabilities could set forth such general truths. Now, if Adam had been depraved at the time of the trial, he would have had two kinds of disabilities, the constant and the inconstant. If one factor of a problem is inconstant, the result of the whole problem is inconstant and uncertain. Thus the trial of Adam, if he had been depraved, would have been of no value for the purpose for which it was intended. It would have established no general truth in regard to all men in connection with the perils of temptation, and the necessity for a Saviour.

114. *Q.* What important event was divided by this official trial?

A. The Creator's revelation of the human moral problem.

115. *Q.* What portion of it preceded the trial?

A. The revelation that the earth contained dangerous elements; that certain of them were destructive to man; that man had a Sovereign who was his Creator; that as Sovereign he commanded that man should not taste or even touch the destructive elements, lest he die, thus making the destructive forbidden. This was the first stage of the presentation of man's moral problem.

116. *Q.* What did the trial of man's representative at this juncture become?

A. It became an object lesson in the revelation of the human moral problem.

117. *Q.* What natural divisions has this object lesson?

A. On the one hand the temptation, and on the other the yielding to the temptation. Each part has a separate and distinct lesson.

118. *Q.* What lesson did the temptation teach?

A. That the destructive, which the Creator had just made forbidden, was attractive to the nature he had given man. This fact, as we have seen, adds immensely to man's moral peril. This was the second stage in the moral problem.

119. *Q.* What grand department of human nature first appeared in the yielding to temptation?

A. Human free agency, or freedom of choice.

120. *Q.* How should propositions containing the element of choice be treated?

A. Very much in the same way that mathematicians treat propositions coming under the theory of probabilities. They are too subtle for human perception. Choice, or free agency, is an element so coy, so timid,

MAN'S FIRST OFFICIAL REPRESENTATIVE. 41

that if the rigid laws of necessity be applied to it, it is frightened away. It seems to be a power to produce effects without a cause, or perhaps it is better to say it is a power of first cause. When this element enters into a question, its answer becomes a matter of probability and not of necessity.

121. *Q.* Can the probability of a choice be expressed in known terms?

A. In some cases it may, but in the more important cases involved in the human moral problem, it cannot. If the inducements are equal, the chance of any one choice is a fraction whose denominator is the number of choices. If a child is offered his choice of two apples that are alike, the chance of either choice is one half. If the number of apples is three, then the chance of each choice is one third. But if the choice is between an apple, a pear, and a piece of coin, the case is very much more complicated, and it would involve so many factors that it would be impossible to express in exact figures the relative probability of each choice. It is possible, however, to determine in which direction the strongest probability lies.

122. *Q.* What was the probability in regard to the first parents eating the forbidden fruit?

A. At the time that the destructive was made forbidden, and before it was found to be attractive, the probability that the first parents would not partake of it was so strong as to amount to almost a certainty. If they had been consulted, they would have said that they would surely not eat that which would be their destruction. When the temptation came, the case was seriously changed. The probability was materially increased in the direction of their partaking. Yet it would hardly seem to an observer whose experience was no greater than that of the first parents, that the probability was actually greater in the direction of partaking, for the inducements were a thousand to one against it.

123. *Q.* What new factor of his moral problem did the yielding to the first temptation bring to the perception of man?

A. The terribly insidious power that pleasure, when it is of the present or near future, even though it be temporary and trifling, has over the free choice of mankind. This closed the object lesson, and is the third part of the revelation of the human moral problem.

124. *Q.* From these three stages in the revelation and history of the moral problem, what seems to have been, at this juncture, the prospects of our first parents?

A. Complete failure in the objects of existence.

125. *Q.* What did Adam thus, as representative, establish for the whole race of man?

A. The strongest kind of probability, though not a necessity, that the whole race would yield to temptation and do the forbidden.

126. *Q.* What did such a strong probability make sure for the race of man?

A. Taken in connection with the fact that once doing the forbidden fixed irrevocable ruin on every one so doing, it made certain the sinking into ruin of the whole race, if it were left to itself.

127. *Q.* What, then, according to our deductions, is the real meaning of the common expression, The fall of man in the fall of Adam?

A. It means the prospective ruin of all men, that was made sure by the test of the first man.

128. *Q.* What was the necessity of thus early demonstrating this gloomy prospect?

A. The revelation of the Saviour was to be made, but it could not fittingly be done until after the demonstration of man's certain ruin without one.

129. *Q.* What was the fourth stage in the presentation of the human moral problem?

A. It was the revelation of this Saviour.

130. *Q.* What do these stages contain?

A. These four stages — the commandment, the temptation, the yielding, and the Saviour — are landmarks within which are comprised the whole human moral problem.

131. *Q.* Who was this Saviour?

A. He is called in revelation the seed of the woman. His name is Jesus Christ. He has been called in the Scriptures by some hundred different names and titles, which bring out the different phases of his personality, his character, and his life-work.

MAN'S SECOND REPRESENTATIVE.

132. *Q.* What name does Paul give him that shows forth a peculiar phase of his work and personality and that throws light on our subject?

A. He calls him the second man, the second Adam, and the last Adam. These all mean the same thing, and show that Paul wished to bring to notice the fact that he had a kind of correspondence with the first Adam.

133. *Q.* In what did this correspondence consist?

A. Man, as a moral and responsible being, had two phases. The first Adam, a representative man, presented the first, and the second Adam, also a representative man, presented the other.

134. *Q.* What were these two phases in manhood?

A. One was man fallen, the other was man upright; one was man doing wrong, the other was man doing right; one was man in the rapids going to destruction, the other was man standing firmly on the rock of safety.

135. *Q.* How did the first Adam bring out the unpropitious phase of manhood?

A. By yielding to temptations in the test case.

136. *Q.* Did the second Adam have a season of temptation that corresponded to that of the first Adam?

A. He had a season of temptation in the commencement of presenting himself in the Messiahship. The localities were the wilderness, the pinnacle of the temple, and the high mount. This experience was to him a private one, as no man was with him; but it must have had more than a private significance, or he would never have reported it so that the world should know it, for it was not like him to make a parade of his private matters. It is eminently fitting to consider this temptation as in contrast to that of the first Adam ; and as its result was victory and good fortune, it brought out the bright phase of manhood in contrast to the dark phase that was the result of the temptation of the first Adam.

137. *Q.* In what light can the second temptation be placed that will prove its significance to man?

A. Let us suppose that it had ended in yielding, as that of the first Adam did, and attempt to measure the magnitude of the fall that man would have had in it. There would then have been no doubt as to its significance to man. The fall of man would have been a thousand times greater than in the other case, since it would have taken man's last hope with it.

138. *Q.* Why was it important that the test temptation of the fall should have a counterpart in the temptations of the Saviour?

A. The test trial of the fall established two important principles, — the terribly insidious power of temptation, and the certainty that man would yield to it. These taken together are the foundation of man's necessity for a Saviour, and it was fitting that the Saviour should make known his power. This he did do in the test trial at the beginning of his ministry, which was probably the most severe that was ever inflicted on human nature, and which seemed to be in correspondence with the earlier trial, that established the necessity of a Saviour. The removal of temptation from the world would have been one kind of salvation. But this trial of the Saviour proves that this is not his method. It also proves that he could enable man, with all his weaknesses and passions, to live upon earth and to resist temptations. He resisted in his own power, and yet he had human passions and weaknesses like the first Adam, who yielded and fell, and like human nature in general. From this we see both the method and the ability of the human Saviour.

139. *Q.* How does the severity of man's two test trials compare with each other?

A. From the scanty history, it would seem that the first was not severe,— no more so than could be looked for in the ordinary human experience. But the other seems to be greater in severity than is ever found in the ordinary, or even the extraordinary experience of men. It seems to have been a season of greater severity of temptation than was ever inflicted on other men, for it was arbitrarily and miraculously made severe.

140. *Q.* What was the purpose of such a contrast in the two trials?

A. The first, in being very weak, showed the weakness and utter helplessness of man without his Saviour. The other made conspicuous the more than sufficiency of the Saviour for man's greatest necessities.

141. *Q.* What other important purpose does the publishing of our Saviour's private struggle with temptation serve?

A. It serves as evidence of his incarnation. The human mind naturally rebels against believing in the incarnation, and the most positive evidence is necessary on that account. Had this private struggle not been divulged, there would have been no positive evidence as to his susceptibility to temptation, — an indispensable attribute of humanity. Elsewhere in his history we find record of his struggles with pain and sorrow, with the treachery and ingratitude of men; but it does not clearly appear that he was beset with temptation to do the forbidden, though that was probably the case.

142. *Q.* What important purpose does the publishing of our Saviour's victory in his private struggle with his temptations serve?

A. After the first Adam had by his fall established the fact that temptation was a power that would ruin men, and the Creator had promised a Saviour for men, it was a natural and logical presumption that that Saviour would remove the temptations which were the source of the ruin. The victory of the second Adam, who was a representative of saved men, dissipates this presumption, and establishes the fact that the Saviour's method of salvation is to give man the power to gain a victory in the midst of and in spite of temptations.

143. *Q.* How can the second Adam be the representative and pattern of saved men, when he was never lost?

A. Being lost is not necessary to salvation. He was a pattern of salvation in its completest sense, for he was saved always from yielding to temptation; he was saved from ever turning in the slightest degree in the direction of being lost. When men are saved who have been lost like the first Adam, they receive power from the Saviour to resist temptation and become like him. It is not necessary that they should become lost in order that he should save them. He is just as well able to give them strength to resist the first temptation as to resist any afterwards. He is able to reinstate those who have become lost, and thus make them victorious like himself; but if there are any who never have become lost, but have always resisted temptation, he is even a greater Saviour to them.

144. *Q.* Are there any such in the flesh?

A. There seems to be no logical difficulty in the existence of such. There is no good reason why the child should not grow into obedience as it grows into responsibility. If such is ever the case, it is due to the power of the Saviour in connection with the authority and judicious instruction of its parents. It is not easy to prove the existence of such cases; but it is no part of reason to deny their existence.

145. *Q.* How does the human nature of the first Adam compare with that of the second?

A. The official character of the first Adam in connection with the moral problem of mankind ended with the fall. Afterwards he was no more than other men, and there is no significance in the comparison beyond that time. The whole life of the second Adam had a significance in the moral problem, but the last three years especially. The first Adam, up to the time of his reverse, was free from all inherited or acquired biases in the wrong direction. The human nature of the second Adam was like that of the first in this respect. The first Adam was up to that time free from all blameworthiness; he was innocent of all wrongdoing. The second Adam was like him in this respect. The innocence of the first Adam was of a negative sort. He was not praiseworthy any more than he was blameworthy, for the reason that he had had no opportunity to become either. At the first opportunity that he had to establish any positive character of any kind, he yielded to the wrong and became blameworthy, and thus ended his official character. The second Adam established positive praiseworthiness of character in the terrible struggle and victory over temptation that he maintained throughout life. The human nature of both the first Adam and the second was susceptible to temptation to do the forbidden. In both cases this susceptibility was a matter disconnected and entirely different from human depravity, that is so broadcast in the rest of the human race.

146. *Q.* What remarkable fact is there in this connection?

A. That these two individuals, who were the only ones that the Creator ever made as individual representatives of the human race, should both of them have been without human depravity, a quality that is so generally, and, as some teach, so universally and so firmly fastened on every other member of the human race.

147. *Q.* In view of these facts, how can the first and the second Adam be proper representatives of depraved humanity?

A. This can only be true on the supposition that human depravity is only an incidental and not a fundamental factor in the great human moral problem.

148. *Q.* What two facts go to prove that human depravity is not a fundamental factor in the moral problem?

A. The first is that the fall of the first man Adam, before he was depraved, proves that there was a sufficient evil tendency in every member of the human family to make sure his fall, without taking into account any force of depravity. The second is, that the second Adam is spoken of in various places in the Scriptures as human, in that he was tempted like other human beings. This could not be true if depravity were fundamental, and anything more than incidental as a force in producing the temptations of men.

149. *Q.* From this light of the subject, what is the natural as well as the logical inference?

A. That depravity has been regarded as a factor of too great magnitude. That much in the evil tendencies of human nature that belongs to man's original susceptibility to temptation has been charged to depravity by religious teachers.

150. *Q.* What does man's earthly environment make of his every appetite, his every passion, his every sentiment, and perhaps his every intellectual faculty?

A. A snare that may lead him to destruction. This is true of all of them, before they are in any way debased or warped from their original type. This is the peril that was shown by the first Adam to make necessary either death or a Saviour. This is the peril in which it was demonstrated by the second Adam that man could live, and in spite of it could flourish. It was this peril, and not human depravity, that was the sole point in the two great object-lessons taught by the first and the second Adam.

151. *Q.* What does depravity never do for man?

A. It does not create any new powers or susceptibilities, nor any new passions or sensibilities. It does not make any new department in human nature, nor does it blot out any. It does not give to any department of human nature its susceptibility to temptation, for where this is found since the advent of depravity, it also existed before that advent.

152. *Q.* What is the effect of depravity upon men?

A. It is great in various ways, but it is not altogether in the way of increasing temptation. It has effect in the belittling of self; it reduces man's standard of being. It may increase the strength of some kinds of temptation, and weaken that of others. It is different in different men. Insanity and idiocy are the goals of aggravated cases, for a drunkard is both insane and idiotic. It weakens the power of choice, and in that way takes away the independence of manhood. It reduces the power of resisting temptations; but though a factor in temptations, it is not the prime nor the principal one. It is caused by yielding to temptation, but it then turns and increases its own cause. It moulds in an unfavorable way both the temptations and the power of choice of him that yields.

153. *Q.* How have many theologians treated human depravity?

A. As the sole cause of human temptation to do the forbidden.

154. *Q.* What patent facts are they obliged to ignore?

A. The fact that the advent of depravity is of a later date in our world than the temptations; the fact that the Saviour was tempted in its absence; and the fact that even depraved humanity must possess the same elements of nature that caused the temptations of our Saviour, or else he was not one of us, and was not tempted like us as the Scriptures declare he was.

155. *Q.* What is the reason why some theologians so unduly and persistently magnify human depravity?

A. It seems to be because they wish to release the Creator from the responsibility of moral evil. Depravity is a creation of man; and whatever of moral evil can be charged to depravity seems to rest upon man, and in this way the Creator seems to be relieved of responsibility.

156. *Q.* Does the Creator thus become relieved?

A. It might seem so if we view only from the surface; but if followed out to the last analysis, it involves him in greater difficulties than those sought to be removed.

157. *Q.* What are these difficulties?

A. It is evident, and needs no proof, that disobedience must antedate depravity in order to be the cause of it. It is equally evident that temptations antedate the disobedience, for men will never do what they have no desires to do. Now, if human depravity is the cause of all temptations, then depravity antedates temptations, and we have a perfect and a beautiful circle. Circles in logic are not like circles in mathematics; in mathematics they are logical enough, but in logic they are not. They destroy and dissipate the whole problem; they bring in the factor absurdity, which destroys every member of the problem found in the circle. This circle would prove the impossible existence of all three, — disobedience, temptation, and depravity, — since they would all antedate and cause each other, which is supreme absurdity. It does not relieve the Creator to involve him in such an absurdity. Again, depravity is possible to man only because his Creator so fashioned him; and if it is the sole cause of man's temptations, and thus of moral evil, then the Creator is just as positively responsible for moral evil as he is on the supposition that he gave him originally the susceptibility to temptation. The difficulty is not removed by being disguised, — by being placed one step farther back. It is impossible to avoid the Creator's sovereignty in the moral evils and the moral problem of man. This sovereignty does not destroy man's free agency, but it does involve him in hardships that try that God-like attribute.

158. *Q.* As touching this matter, what do truth and candor compel us to believe?

A. That the Creator originally and purposely gave man a nature that was susceptible to temptation, that he also gave him free agency, and that he also did this in spite of the fact that he knew it would insure the ruin of many, though the Saviour were free to all.

159. *Q.* Are the Creator's plans and methods in harmony with perfect justice and love?

A. We say and believe that they are.

160. *Q.* Can we make this harmony appear in all departments of creation?

A. We cannot; we may do it in general, but not in particular cases. It is easy for us to conceive, and perhaps to perceive, that the Creator's plans accomplish the greatest good for the greatest numbers; but our ideas of eminent domain are such that we instinctively feel that if the individual gives up or suffers for the general good, he should in some way receive a compensation. We see in our world much individual suffering in the interest of our Creator's great plan for the good of man as a whole. This suffering is partly deserved and partly undeserved. There is no possible way that these sufferers can receive compensation in this world; but we hope, and often say, that these things will be made all right in the world to come. This world to come is, however, so misty and impenetrable, that we are obliged to leave this matter of harmony in individual cases simply resting upon hope.

161. *Q.* As touching the moral problem of man, what are the two great and vital questions?

A. What are man's necessities, and how does the Saviour that is offered for him meet these necessities.

162. *Q.* What are man's necessities?

A. We have seen, in the progress of our analysis, that man's peril upon earth is his frightful tendency to do the forbidden, which is destructive to him. There are two different necessities growing out of this peril. We have seen that this tendency is so great and insidious that a large number of the race (some theologians say there are no exceptions) will some time in their lives surely yield to it. We have also seen that once doing the forbidden infects the nature with a moral disease that eventually produces ruin, in spite of every human power to prevent it. Thus comes the necessity of a supernatural power, to purge man of such infection. But man has another necessity. There is very little of true salvation in oft-repeated infection and cure, in a continual falling and being lifted up. Man needs a supernatural strength to offset the insidious power of temptation.

PREVENTION AS DISTINGUISHED FROM CURE.

163. *Q.* What is the grand distinction in these two necessities?

A. One is the cure of moral disease, and the other is the prevention of it.

164. *Q.* Which is the more fundamental and important in man's salvation?

A. It is evident that prevention is; for a state of complete prevention from moral disease is salvation itself. Cure is always a necessity when prevention is not complete. When prevention has been complete from the first, cure does not become a necessity, as was true of the great Physician himself. Prevention is the end; a cure may be the means to the end, but nothing more, and it is of value only as it contributes to the end, which is the exemption from disease. Prevention is thus fundamental, while cure is incidental.

165. *Q.* What important matters are indissolubly connected with the incidental in man's salvation?

A. Repentance, conversion, regeneration, atonement, and others.

166. *Q.* How can it be shown that all these important matters are only incidental to Christian life and salvation?

A. The most perfect Christian character that ever lived was perfect in the absence of them. He was the great pattern for men to follow, and thus these factors become man's necessity because he does not follow his pattern. If there are any that follow their pattern from the first, these incidental factors are no more necessary for them than they were for the pattern Christ.

167. *Q.* Did the Saviour need a Saviour?

A. The same susceptibility to temptation that the Creator saw fit to place in human nature was likewise in the human nature of Christ. His environment, especially at the time of his official trial, seemed to be prepared to intensify that susceptibility, and he needed superhuman power to prevent his yielding to this temptation. He found that power in his own deific self. His necessity for a Saviour was of the fundamental kind, and is always found in every man, both Christian and otherwise. It is that which always adheres to man in the flesh. The other necessity which is incidental to fallen man was not found in Christ.

168. *Q.* How is the human necessity for a Saviour made manifest by the official trials of the first and second Adam?

A. A trial, or test, whether of men or things, is always, in a strict sense, ordered to find out or to set forth attributes which existed before the trial, and not those that the result of the trial may originate. The first official trial in which all men were represented did set forth that dangerous susceptibility to temptation with which the Creator saw fit to invest human nature. The result of the trial set forth the fact that if human nature was left to its own resources, it would surely go to ruin and moral death. Thus did temptation and the yielding set forth only that fundamental necessity of a supernatural power to enable them to resist temptation, that adheres to all men, whether fallen or not fallen. But the effect of the trial originated in man a moral disease, or excrescence, which did not exist before, and which the Creator did not implant in human nature. The Creator did not give to human nature itself the power to cure or remove this disease. Hence arose our second necessity. The second official trial only set forth man's fundamental necessity for a Saviour, and this still more vividly than did the first. The second necessity, which we have termed incidental, had no connection with the second trial, for the second trial did not set forth the necessity for a Saviour to forgive.

169. *Q.* What, then, is the parallel between man's two necessities for a superhuman Saviour, — the one to preserve him blameless, and the other to forgive him?

A. The one is the creation of God, the other of man; the one emanates from human nature in its healthy normal state, the other from human nature when it has become diseased and abnormal; the one the Creator intended to be a fixture, the other need never have been, and may be done away with; the one was present in Paradise with the pure natures of the first parents, the advent of the other was of a later date; the one was not lost, though the other was born, when Paradise was lost; the one will still live in Paradise regained, the other will disappear when Paradise is completely regained; the one was in the humanity of the Saviour, the other was always a stranger to it. For these reasons we may regard the one as fundamental and the other as incidental.

170. *Q.* How can that be incidental which the Scriptures made so prominent?

A. It is the grand starting-point in a change of life and character, and is all important for that reason. Man has generally made it a necessity unto himself, yet he is able to place himself above that necessity, as did the first Great Example. But he can never rise above that other necessity, for even the Great Example himself did not. The Lord's Prayer notices both of man's necessities, — forgiveness of trespasses and deliverance from temptation. When the deliverance from yielding to temptation is complete, the necessity for a Saviour to forgive is concluded. The Master himself was thus delivered.

171. *Q.* John said, "Behold the Lamb of God, that taketh away the sins of the world." What could John have meant by this?

A. It seems to be something deeper and more fundamental than pardoning the sins of the world. It seems to strike the sins themselves, and to reduce the very causes that have made the Saviour a necessity for the world. The hand of God prevents disobedience.

172. *Q.* How can the Lamb of God take away the sin of the world?

A. He can do it by imparting to men the power he manifested, as second Adam, in resisting temptation.

173. *Q.* Why is not this power, which was sufficient for the Christ, all-sufficient for all other men?

A. It would be, if all men would avail themselves of it and resist temptation from the first. But they do not; and they thus bring a new factor into the moral problem that was not implanted in it by the Creator in the first place. We have already noticed that once going astray sows in the nature the seeds of corruption that future well-doing will not remove. In this way each individual man creates for himself a necessity for a supernatural Saviour, that was not an attribute of his original nature.

174. *Q.* Did not the fall of Adam bring upon man his necessity for a Saviour?

A. No; we have seen that man has two different necessities for a Saviour,—the one natural and the other artificial. The natural was his need of power to insure his resistance to temptation; the other was his need of a power for his regeneration after he had yielded to temptation. The natural existed before the fall; the artificial, Adam brought upon himself by the transgression of the fall; but he did not bring it upon any one else. Each person brings upon himself his own necessity for a Saviour for his own forgiveness and regeneration.

175. *Q.* What connection had the trial and the fall of the first Adam with human necessities for a Saviour?

A. The trial and the fall established the attractiveness of the forbidden to human nature of such a magnitude as to necessitate a superhuman Saviour. This necessity the Creator made inherent in human nature, and it was outside of man's power of choice. The fall and its immediate consequences brought to light another necessity for a Saviour that was within the province of human choice, that Adam had brought upon himself, and that the whole of his issue would probably bring upon themselves. This was the necessity of one that could take away the guilt and the penalty for actual transgressions.

176. *Q.* From the way that many religious teachers set forth this subject, what are some of the inferences that would be forced upon us?

A. (1) That man's principal and fundamental necessity is a supernatural Saviour, to take away the guilt and the penalty of his wrong-doing; (2) That this necessity was brought upon all men by the transgressions of the first parents in the garden; (3) That the fall of the first parents entailed upon every individual of the race, in advance of his existence, a kind of disability or corruption that made his salvation impossible without supernatural intervention; (4) That the fall caused all the tendencies to wrong-doing that we see in mankind; (5) That all the suffering and death of our Saviour was laid upon him on account of the evil deeds of men.

177. *Q.* What may be said in regard to the first inference?

A. It requires no argument to show that man's greatest good and highest attainment is to be like his Saviour, perfect in obedience. It follows that man's greatest necessity is of a power sufficient to insure such an attainment. If man in himself is sufficient to insure it, then he has no need of foreign assistance. But the trial of the first Adam proves otherwise. Man's greatest and fundamental necessity is of a Saviour who can enable him to be like Jesus, perfect in obedience. Forgiveness and removal of guilt is a necessity for those who have once gone astray, as a means toward the great end, — obedience. It is, however, incidental, because it is not a necessity for those who never go astray. There was one such man, the God-man, and there is no logical reason why there should not be others. Therefore man's fundamental necessity is for supernatural power to enable him to be like the Saviour, obedient. This kind of necessity was his before he had brought upon himself another necessity by his disobedience. It continued his after he had gone astray, and had brought upon himself the necessity of one to reinstate him; and it is still adhering to him after his guilt is washed away, and he is a new creature.

178. *Q.* What absurdity springs out of making the washing away of guilt and the removing of the penalty the whole function of our Saviour?

A. We are told in the Scripture that there is no other name whereby we can be saved. Now, if there are any who do not go astray and bring upon themselves guilt, such cannot be saved, because his function does not reach them.

179. *Q.* What standard statement is always ready, and supposed to be equal to dissolving this difficulty?

A. It is said that every man goes astray; commits guilty acts that necessitate the function of a Saviour.

180. *Q.* Does this statement dissolve the difficulty?

A. No; cure is not health. To the sick, cure is a necessity. In their case it is only a means to promote health, and is of value only to the degree that it tends to promote health. They have the best health who have no necessity for a cure, and that is the highest function of a physician which can so prescribe for a healthy patient as to exclude the necessity for a cure. The Great Physician is incidentally able to cure the sin-sick, but his highest function is to prescribe for the morally healthy, so that they need not become sin-sick. His own humanity, through his divine skill, was always preserved in this way. If it were possible to prove that all become morally diseased and need the curative power of the Great Physician, it would not take away their necessity for that higher function. Unless the Great Physician can prescribe for those whom he has cured of sin-sickness, as well as for those who are always morally well, so as to confirm and establish their health, he is not equal to the necessities of man. Unless he can preserve blameless as well as forgive, he is not a sufficient nor an efficient Saviour for man.

181. *Q.* What may be said in regard to the second inference in question 176?

A. They tell us that God created man in his own image, holy; that by the transgression of the fall he became guilty, and brought upon himself a tendency to wrong-doing; that he thus lost the image of God, and hence arose the necessity of a Saviour for him. In reply, it may be said that God did make man in his own image; but this image consisted in an intellectual as well as a moral nature. God could not create man holy, in a positive sense, any more than he could create him guilty. Man did not lose the image of God in the fall; he retains his intellectual and moral powers after he is guilty. The fall made no one guilty but the first parents, who transgressed. It did not originate in them their tendency to wrong-doing, for this tendency existed before the fall; else the fall would have been an impossibility. Man is lost, not on account of his tendency to wrong-doing, but when he commits his free agency to wrong-doing. Each individual is lost on account of the wrong use of his own free agency, and not on account of that of the first parents. Hence the transgressions of the first parents in the garden did not bring upon men their necessities for a Saviour.

182. *Q.* What may be said in regard to the third inference in question 176?

A. We have already seen that the first parents had no greater power to transmit their attributes, whether natural or artificial, to their descendants, than other human parents have; for if they had, either they or others would not have been human. The first parents could not carry disabilities many generations. Therefore the third inference arises from a false position.

183. *Q.* What can be said in regard to the fourth inference in question 176?

A. That the fall of our first parents caused all the tendencies to wrong-doing that we see in mankind, seems to follow from much that has been written. It is, however, two stages away from the truth. In the first place, the test case of the fall, though initiating the depravity that we see broadcast in the world, was not the cause of it. Second, if it had been the cause of depravity, it would not have been the cause of the tendencies seen in mankind to wrong-doing, for depravity is secondary. The primary cause of human peril is the nature given to man by the Creator, and is still seen at a later date in the human nature of Him who was tempted like as we are, but with no trace of depravity in his nature.

184. *Q.* What may be said in regard to the fifth inference of question 176?

A. That the sufferings and death of Christ were necessary to constitute him a forgiving Saviour, we do not deny. But we do deny that the forgiving power was the whole of his function as man's Saviour. We have tried to prove that he is a Saviour in a far more important and fundamental sense than that of the taking away of the guilt and penalty of wrong-doing. John seems to bring out this important side of the Saviour's power when he says, " Behold the Lamb of God that taketh away the sin of the world." This is more generic than taking away the guilt and penalty of evil deeds. It is taking away the evil deeds themselves, and in that way reduces the necessity of the forgiving function. That the Saviour is actually reducing the evil deeds of men no one will deny. No one who believes Christianity will deny that the despised Nazarene is at the bottom of the wiping away of the slavery of the middle ages, and that he has been and always will be at the bottom of every high attainment of mankind. Obedience is the foundation of every high attainment. Christ is the power that enables man to be obedient, and it is only through his suffering and death that he acquired this power.

185. *Q.* What theory is frequently held in connection with the removal of depravity?

A. That the near approach of the death of a Christian either enables or makes the Saviour willing to remove the last vestige of depravity from him, so that he can enter into the new world completely saved.

186. *Q.* What are the grounds for such a theory?

A. Scarcely more than those arising from the necessities connected with what we have endeavored to prove are false conceptions of human depravity. The idea is frequently held that depravity is blameworthy, and no person possessing any vestige of it can be in a state of perfect obedience. This doctrine, taken in connection with the fact that there is no offer of forgiveness except in this world, seemed to preclude the salvation of any; and from this arose the doctrine of the removal of depravity at the approach of death.

187. *Q.* What shall we say to this doctrine?

A. That the presumption is against it; that the Scriptures give no evidence for it, and that the strongest proof must be given before we should accept it.

188. *Q.* What, according to our deductions, is a partial solution of the problem here involved?

A. The doctrine seems to rest upon the idea that perfect obedience is not possible as long as there is any depravity. We claim, however, that this is not true. Depravity seems to be an encumbrance to perfect obedience, but not a bar. Depravity seems to be no more of a bar than is the original weakness with which the Creator saw fit to invest man. Salvation is obedience, and complete salvation is perfect obedience, and can be nothing less. But the Saviour's method does not seem to be that of removing either the weakness or the depravity at once. Unless the Saviour can assist man to perfect obedience, he is imperfect as a Saviour. Perfect obedience, however, does not demand choices beyond attainments; it does not demand acts of brilliancy beyond one's light; to act up to one's light is perfect obedience. And this sort of a life may be found in true Christians in this world long before death. Depravity may be of so grievous a kind as to destroy accountability. Those who are depraved to this extent are no longer moral beings; they are negatives, neither obedient nor disobedient.

189. *Q.* What has been the cause of much of the ambiguity in the presentation of truths connected with the human moral problem?

A. The many meanings which have been given to the word "sin."

190. *Q.* What are these meanings?

A. The primary meaning is disobedience to the Creator's laws; and it would be better if the word had no other meaning. But religious teachers use the word in other ways. King James's Version uses it with different meanings, and Webster's Dictionary recognizes them. One meaning is temptation to disobedience; another is susceptibility to temptation; still another is human depravity. It is used in the sense of the shortcomings of weakness and infirmity. It is also used to signify disobedience in the abstract,—an idea that is better expressed in the phrase that we have used,— the forbidden.

191. *Q.* What does the word "sin" always suggest?

A. Guilt.

192. *Q.* Does guilt belong to sin?

A. Never, except when used in its primary sense. There is no guilt in temptation, nor in susceptibility to temptation, nor in depravity, nor in the shortcomings of weakness and infirmity. There is no guilt in the forbidden before it becomes connected with the free moral agent.

193. *Q.* What should theologians and religious teachers do?

A. They should restrict the word "sin" to those acts to which responsibility and guilt unmistakably belong. Much of the controversy concerning Christian attainments is brought about by one party restricting the word in this way, and the other embracing in it the shortcomings of weakness and infirmity, to which guilt no more belongs than it does to the stumbling of the blind man or the limping of the cripple. Many discourses on the dreadful guilt of sin lose their effect, since the speaker uses the word in various senses, only one of which has the least shade of guilt attached to it.

194. *Q.* What has generally been made the fundamental cause of man's necessity for the supernatural power of the God-man?

A. The fact that man is a "sinner."

195. *Q.* What was formerly the meaning of the word "sinner" in this connection?

A. The word referred not only to the actual guilt of each transgressor, but also to an inherited guilt that each one was supposed to have acquired from Adam. Each person was therefore supposed to be subject to punishment, not only on account of his own guilt, but also on account of the guilt of Adam.

196. *Q.* What is the modern meaning of the word "sinner" in this connection?

A. An actual transgressor, and generally something more. Although modern teachers do not say that the first parents transmitted their own guilt to all their issue, they still sometimes teach that the first parents did fasten some sort of a misty disability on their issue, — a disability that gives rise to the necessity of a Saviour, and which the Saviour must remove in order to produce complete salvation.

197. *Q.* What, according to our deductions, is the fundamental cause of man's necessity for the supernatural power of the God-man?

A. It is man's extreme liability to do the forbidden that is so destructive to him. We would not detract in the least from man's necessity of one to take away his guilt after he has actually done the forbidden; but we regard this as a means to an end, which end is complete obedience.

198. *Q.* Is the removal of depravity a necessity unto salvation?

A. According to our deductions it is not. Salvation is complete when obedience is complete. Obedience tends to wipe out depravity, but it does not do so at once; it acts gradually. And it can never remove man's original liability to temptation, which, as we have seen, is fundamental in his nature.

199. *Q.* What seems to have been an error in much religious teaching?

A. It has been the confounding of man's tendency to do the forbidden with the actual doing of the forbidden, and thus making it a necessity that this tendency should be removed in order that salvation should be complete. This our Saviour, in his own person, has clearly demonstrated not to be true.

200. *Q.* What factor in human moral necessities for a Saviour have some writers on systematic theology generally overlooked or treated as of little importance?

A. It is the susceptibility to the attractiveness of the forbidden, with which the Creator originally saw fit to invest human nature. It is seen in its purity before the advent of depravity at the fall, and also in the nature of the Incarnate One during his whole stay on earth; and it is present in every other human nature, more or less mixed with the artificial disability, — human depravity.

THE END.

www.ingramcontent.com/pod-product-compliance
Lightning Source LLC
Chambersburg PA
CBHW022152090426
42742CB00010B/1476